DRIVING LESSONS

Christian meditations about life from the not-so-fast lane

by
SHARON ELWELL

illustrated by
LAFE LOCKE

mp
MERIWETHER PUBLISHING LTD.
Colorado Springs, Colorado

Meriwether Publishing Ltd., Publisher
P.O. Box 7710
Colorado Springs, CO 80933

Editors: Arthur L. Zapel, Rhonda Wray
Typesetting: Sharon E. Garlock
Cover design and cartoon illustrations: Lafe Locke
Art direction: Tom Myers

© Copyright MCMXCV Meriwether Publishing Ltd.
Printed in the United States of America
First Edition

Library of Congress Cataloging-in-Publication Data

Elwell, Sharon, 1943-
    Driving lessons : Christian meditations about life from the not-so-fast lane / by Sharon Elwell.
    p. cm.
    ISBN 1-56608-009-6
    1. Christian life—Meditations.   2. Christian life—Humor.
    3. Elwell, Sharon, 1943- —Anecdotes. I. Title.
BV501.2.E437 1994
242—dc20   94-47507
                                               CIP

CONTENTS

PART ONE
SINGLE PASSENGER VEHICLE

  1. Yield 3

  2. Me vs. Everybody 6

  3. Following Too Closely 9

  4. Rattles, Smoke, and Moments of Grace 12

  5. Running From the Wreck 15

  6. Witness 18

  7. Intersection 21

  8. Pharisee on the Freeway 24

PART TWO
CHECKING THE MANUAL

  9. Objects in This Mirror 29

  10. Let Your Light So Shine 32

  11. License 35

  12. Dirty Windshield 38

  13. Setting Up the Idle 41

  14. The Safety Zone 44

  15. Speed Limits 47

  16. Asking for Directions 50

  17. Reading the Map 53

  18. Staying out of the Way 57

PART THREE
LOOKING OUT THE WINDOW

19. Stuck in Line *63*

20. Brownian Motion and Mexican Taxi Drivers . . . *66*

21. The Designated Driver *69*

22. Respect *72*

23. My Very First Accident! *75*

24. Talking Your Way Through *78*

25. It's On Fire! It's My Car! *81*

26. The Gift *84*

27. Nervous in the Choir *87*

28. Out of Gas *90*

29. Into the Cow Pasture *93*

PART FOUR
SHARING THE ROAD

30. Just Like a Cadillac *99*

31. The Carpool Lane *101*

32. Slow Down for Children *104*

33. Jericho Road *107*

34. Gridlock *110*

35. Blind Spots *113*

36. Signals *116*

37. The Guy Behind Me *119*

38. Driving Well *122*

39. Killing With Kindness *125*

40. Rush Hour Harmony *128*

About the Author *131*

To My Daughters

Okay, so I wasn't the best driving teacher in the world. A little nervous. A little too quick to gasp and stomp the floor on the passenger side, where there really should be a brake. Each of you in turn complained to your dad about that hissing sound I made sucking air in over my teeth, trying not to pass out from terror.

I suppose you grew up to drive well in spite of me. Letting someone you love choose their own road and steer their course is not an easy business. Now that some of you are parents, you're learning that for yourselves. But I definitely gained something from the experience. I learned to pay attention.

The road, especially the freeway, is dangerous. One lapse can cause you to miss a turn and find yourself many miles from where you had hoped to be. And so many skills are required! You must know how to get in gear, to speed up, to slow down, to yield, to merge, even to reverse yourself from time to time.

Fortunately, there are exciting discoveries to be made everywhere — even on the freeway. These are some of mine. You won't have any trouble finding your own. All you have to do is steer your own vehicle, choose your road, and remember to pay attention.

For God hath not given us the spirit of fear, but of power, and of love, and of a sound mind.

—2 Timothy 1:7 (KJV)

SINGLE PASSENGER VEHICLE

1

YIELD

I understand the concept. I know that I don't have to stop or change direction or abandon my objectives. It's just that someone else has the right to go before me and I need to slow down a little, just enough to let the other car go first. I really do understand the concept. But I can't do it.

Some mechanism in my brain is reversed. When I see a "Yield" sign and another driver coming to the same spot at the same time, I invariably think, "Oh, good! He's going to yield." Then I pull out in front of him.

Only after the near-collision do I remember that I'm supposed to yield. You'd think that one hair-raising narrow escape would be sufficient, but it happens again and again. It seems that I'm always looking in the rearview mirror at some angry driver, grateful that I can't understand whatever it is he's yelling. But the experience, no matter what level of terror I reach, doesn't seem to be powerful enough to overcome my programming. Even after it has been clearly shown that what I've learned is not useful on the road of life, it remains in place, controlling my actions.

It worries me to realize that this one can't possibly be the only glitch in my mental machinery. There are bound to be others. I live according to programming installed years ago, and not all of it has application now. For example, I know how to work a wringer washing machine, "sprinkle down" an ironing with a cork sprinkler stuck in a 7UP bottle, hang a shirt on the line so the clothespin marks don't show. I know how to sift flour, tat, and darn a sock. This information isn't wrong, just not very useful anymore.

But I also learned some things that are wrong. Stereotypes, misconceptions. Trouble is, they feel right to me. I can't recognize the mistakes in my own programming until some other driver shakes a fist at me and points out that I need to rethink. I guess I'm grateful when someone goes to all the trouble to do that. If I don't learn to yield the right-of-way to others, for instance, it could cost my life.

...yielding pacifieth great offenses.

—*Ecclesiastes 10:4 (KJV)*

ME VS. EVERYBODY

I admit it. I love to compete. I'd like to blame my parents or those sixth grade spelling bees, but it's nobody's fault. I'm an old lady who hates to be the last one off the stoplight. I sit tense, foot on the accelerator, eye on the light facing the other way so that I'll be ready as soon as it turns yellow.

You wouldn't think I'd be so competitive, since I never win at anything. For one thing, I don't like to go over the speed limit. As soon as the other driver gets up to speed, the race is over. Still, that first block or so is always a thrill.

I win every time. If I don't, I just make new rules. If nothing else, I can smirk at someone whose car is dirtier than mine, or whose registration is due to expire sooner. There's always a way to feel superior if you look hard enough. It's a skill I developed while the rest of the world was getting chosen for the baseball team. The great thing about competition is that there's always a way to win.

But even when it's fun, competition gives a false sense of accomplishment. If you beat another car into the empty spot in the lane ahead, or pass someone slower to gain a car length, it may feel as if some kind of progress has been made. You're better off than you were, certainly better off than the guy who's still behind you. Except that at the next stoplight he lazily pulls up next to you, relaxed, maybe yawning and changing the radio station, thinking of other things. When you look at him in annoyance, he notices the light change before you do and pulls ahead.

Have you lost? You're no farther from home. Competitive gains and losses deceive us into thinking we have gained or lost something real. There is no actual difference between the Olympic skier who won and the girl who came in .007 slower, except that one is crying tears of joy and the other one is just plain crying.

7

Miss America with her crown is in no respect more beautiful than any of the young women in the line behind her, trying to smile. Believing in those kinds of comparisons has left forty-nine out of fifty girls feeling less beautiful than they had been just minutes before. The trouble with competition is that there's always a way to lose, too.

If a man digs a pit, he will fall into it...

—*Proverbs 26:27*

FOLLOWING TOO CLOSE

The single greatest cause of accidents is following other people too closely.

Driver's Training Manual

California Department of Motor Vehicles

The northern California coast highway takes the driver to beautiful places. The trouble is, you can't look at the beautiful places. You are too busy trying to stay on the road. The fact that you are in the middle of a giant postcard is little consolation when you have to stare at the yellow line, dizzy from leaning left then leaning right, around and around the treacherous curves, shifting gears, trying not to notice the rocky cliffs below or think about the driver who took that last marker out. Had he gone over the edge?

Sometimes the road veers inland through redwood groves. These provide an eerie sense of timelessness and majesty. But it's hard to enjoy timelessness and majesty while you're driving. The sun never makes its way down through this tall old forest. The driver must stay focused, occupied, trying to figure out the road ahead, but unable to see beyond the next curve. There is a constant feeling that a clearing full of sunshine is just ahead. But right now you need headlights.

Alone at twilight not long ago, I was hurrying down the coast when I overtook a pickup. I was happy to find another person going the same direction on this perilous road. In just a few miles, it became obvious that he was an experienced driver, accustomed to all the turns that were so unfamiliar to me. He knew how to straighten out the curves by moving toward the center line, then closer to the edge. He knew how to save his brakes by shifting down and slowing the car before he got to the sharp curves, not after he was already into them.

Suddenly, my journey was easier. I had fewer decisions to make. I could follow this guy. I could speed up if he speeded up, confident that we were heading into a straightaway and not about to hurtle over a cliff at an unexpected turn. I could take his lead, glance at the scenery from time to time, enjoy the sunset. Life was good.

I became so accustomed to following that when he signaled a left turn and slowed down, I signaled too. Then he disappeared into a narrow dirt road and I had to stop myself from tagging along. I actually had to say to myself, "Wait a minute. I don't want to leave the highway. I don't know where he's going." He was just gone, and I was alone in the deepening darkness with many miles left to travel.

For an instant, I felt panic. But I had the map, the road signs, and a clearly marked highway in front of me. I was well-equipped to reach the destination I had chosen for myself. I could get home. And I had to.

The DMV manual says the single greatest cause of accidents is following too closely. I'm not surprised.

"Cursed is the one who trusts in man..."

—*Jeremiah 17:5*

11

RATTLES, SMOKE,
AND MOMENTS OF GRACE

I was ashamed of my first response when I heard the terrible rattling sound at the stoplight: "Oh, no! I hope that's not my car!"

All of us waiting at the light were suddenly enveloped in smoke. I checked my gauges; the car wasn't overheated. Surely it would be overheated if it were on fire, wouldn't it? I rolled down the window and listened carefully.

It was then that I noticed the faces in the other cars. All right, wait a minute. If I hoped the expensive-sounding noise wasn't coming from my car, just exactly whose car did I want it to be coming from? Whom would I select as the recipient of automotive disaster? The mom in the van behind me with a carload of kids in soccer uniforms? The low rider full of Mexican field workers with exhausted, dirty faces? The smug-looking computer nerd in the Saab? Was I going to say a quick prayer for my personal welfare and hope that trouble came to one of them instead?

I was on my way home from a hospital visit that had taught me something. My beautiful friend had looked so tiny and frail in the huge bed that I was wracked with sorrow at the cancer that was ravaging her. "Why you?" I had whispered. She was disappointed at my attitude, and took my hand. "Hey, why not me? I've got to take my lumps like everybody else."

Going past wrecks of all kinds, I've heard people remark, "There, but for the grace of God, go I!" I really hate that idea. The implication that we have been saved from distress because God likes us better than the other guy seems both wrong-headed and mean-spirited. I'm pretty sure the grace of God belongs to everyone. It was with my friend in her hospital bed, and I have seen it with others in equally perilous places, even in death. It dawned on me that the things that cause us fear may not always be bad, but fear can keep us from living well if we give it control over our actions.

I should have known better than to exclude those around me and hope to maintain my personal well-being sitting at the smoke-filled intersection and looking at the other drivers. I mustered a good wish: I hope it's not your car making that noise! The smoke dissipated, and we all drove away. There, by the grace of God, go all of us.

...whoever gloats over disaster will not go unpunished.

—Proverbs 17:5

RUNNING FROM THE WRECK

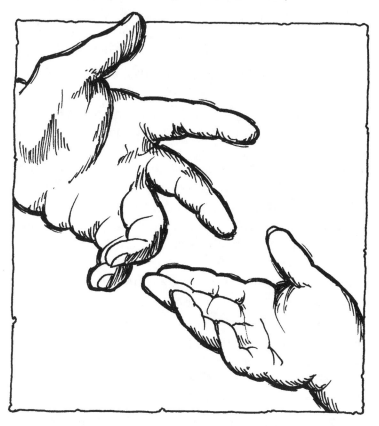

Afterwards, I wondered what had overcome me that dark night when I sped past the wrecked car. What kept me from acting like a citizen, like a Christian? Like myself?

I was alone, it was late, and the road was twisting and perilous. There was no place to pull over. If I stopped in the dark, I would be in danger of getting hit if someone else came by. The people in the car wrapped around the tree may have been beyond my help. They may have already been in an ambulance rushing to the hospital. I didn't know. I couldn't see inside the car. I had no supplies. My first-aid certificate had expired. We were many miles from a telephone. I would call the emergency number at the first stop. My list of excuses was long. I was afraid.

My dad first noticed this phenomenon when he developed lung cancer and everyone around him knew that he would soon die. There was an end to idle chit-chat about baseball and politics. No one told him jokes. People's voices softened when he came near, animated conversations drifted off, people themselves drifted off. No one sought his company anymore. He was death, and all the things that had made him fun to talk to were overridden by that. He said that if he'd known how people would react, he'd never have told anyone his trouble.

When my friend divorced, she found herself sitting alone at church. Her happily married friends didn't call her for lunch, and couples never asked her for dinner anymore. Frustrated, she asked, "Do they think it's contagious?" Yes! Oh, yes indeed!

People with visible physical disabilities report that passersby most often avert their eyes rather than start up a conversation. Sitting in front of her dorm on a college campus, my friend who is blind became increasingly disheartened as students stopped to chat with her dog. None spoke to her, though the Lab quickly acquired dozens of friends.

Another friend's son went to jail. The incident

was in the newspaper, and we live in a small town. No one said a word to her, though she knew people had read about the disaster. She commented later that she had desperately wished for someone to talk with during those lonely, terrible days.

There is a human tendency to affiliate upward, to seek the company of those who seem well and strong and safe so that we feel well and strong and safe, too. It takes courage and commitment to stand beside those who are awkward, lonely, disabled, depressed, weakened, touched by disease or death.

I hope I remember the Savior's example the next time I seek only wonderful, cheerful friends to sit with and talk to. Maybe if I stay at your side when you wreck your vehicle, you won't run from me when I find myself stranded beside the road some dark night.

Have no fear of sudden disaster or of the ruin that overtakes the wicked, for the Lord will be your confidence and will keep your foot from being snared.

—Proverbs 3:25, 26

WITNESS

Important things sometimes come upon us suddenly, while our attention is distracted. I was on the way home from a children's chorus afternoon, my van full of kids, my thoughts full of errands, when I saw the attack. A mailman had been jumped by a group of young people. He was down; they were pummeling him. One had taken the mail sack and was hurrying through the bundles, tossing letters everywhere. My small children and I were terribly alarmed. I was blocks from the nearest public telephone — it was just as close to drive directly to the police station, so I did. At top speed.

Breathless, I rushed in the front door to tell what I knew. Their questions were direct and to the point. Not a second was wasted.

What corner? I hadn't looked. I think it was Franklin. Franklin and Elm. Or is that Pine? By the big green house around the corner from the school.

What were the young people driving? A van. A van of some kind.

What kind? A big van, like a delivery service.

What color? I think it was yellow. Maybe yellow.

License number? I should've noticed that. That's something I really should've noticed. I just didn't take the time. I was anxious to get here as quickly as possible.

How many were there? Oh, there were quite a few. I'm not exactly sure. I didn't think to count. Six or seven. Eight or nine.

Girls or boys? All boys, I think.

What were they wearing? Well, blue clothing, basically blue like jeans. I remember some jeans.

I was a useless witness. My tire-squealing, kid-terrifying drive to the police station was wasted. By the time the patrol car arrived, the kids were dispersed, the mailman was unconscious, and no one else had seen the incident. As the only witness, I had rushed to share what I knew. Trouble was, I didn't know anything. I hadn't taken the time to watch and learn before I tried to give information to others. My testimony should have been the source of information important to the welfare of our community. I hope in the future it will be.

"...for this reason I was born, and for this I came into the world, to testify to the truth."

—John 18:37

INTERSECTION

Life is full of drama when you're sixteen. Learning to drive feels like the most important event taking place in the community — maybe the world. The thrill of successful endeavor is overwhelming. So is the grueling certainty of public mistakes. Sweaty palms on the steering wheel, avoiding the eyes of the man you just cut off, so many things to think about at once, so much power!

My grandmother was the designated person-with-a-license. It was just a formality, of course. I was only a couple of weeks away from my own license. I certainly didn't need anyone to ride along. But in deference to my mother and the laws of the state of California, Grandma rode shotgun. She brought her own style to the task.

I was seriously confused about the brake and the clutch. More than once, I pushed in the clutch expecting to slow the car, and found myself screeching through a turn, trying not to look as surprised and terrified as I felt. On the worst of those occasions, I released the clutch when I suddenly realized it was the wrong pedal. The car jerked to a sudden stop, crosswise in a busy intersection at 5:30 p.m.

Fumbling to start up again, I quickly flooded the engine. The smell of gasoline filled the car. We weren't going anywhere for a few minutes. Neither was anyone else. I didn't think I could endure the humiliation. I couldn't look at the faces behind the windshields.

Grandma, on the other hand, had bigger things on her mind. "I just don't want to cook broccoli if we're going to have a green salad and then lime Jell-O with cottage cheese in it. No dinner ought to be that green. Don't you think raw carrots is plenty for a vegetable?"

"I think so."

"So do I. Well, let's get home and get to work on it."

The car started right up. We were on the way home in seconds. Life is full of unintended bumps, jolts, and potentially embarrassing stalls. No problem. Smart woman, my grandma. The carrots were really all that was needed.

A cheerful heart is good medicine...

—*John 17:22*

PHARISEE ON THE FREEWAY

Beneath this stone lies Dennis O'Day

Who died defending his right of way.

His cause was just; his will was strong.

But he's just as dead as if he'd been wrong.

I've had the fact that I am a Pharisee by inclination demonstrated to me many times. I love the rules. I love knowing the rules and pointing out when they've been violated. Knowing where the commas go is a very big comfort in an uncertain world.

If it were up to me, no kid with a broken leg would be allowed to bat and then choose someone else to run his bases for him. Nine items in the Express Lane means nine items. No counting two boxes of detergent as one item. The apostrophe in *it's* - the contraction - can't be left out, regardless of how frequently you see it improperly used. There's no such word as "brang." No white shoes between Labor Day and Memorial Day. The woman will choose whether to shake hands with the man or not. Serve from the left, pass to the right. "This is she," not "This is me."

A true Pharisee will sit in front of a red light in the dead of night with no car coming in any direction for miles. We're law-abiding types, whether it makes any sense or not. And you don't find us walking into a pedestrian lane against a red light, even if we're alone on the street. Red means red.

We Pharisees are unusually disconcerted when there's a cop in the intersection, waving us through against the light. Has he checked the traffic behind him? Is he sure? Where's his authority? We're likely to take badge numbers. For us, nothing is more unsettling than a change in the rules, particularly on scant authority. Offer Isaac, the only son, on the altar in spite of all the commandments prohibiting child sacrifice? Let the adulteress go unstoned? I don't think so.

And if I have the right-of-way, you'd better let me through. I'll pull out my DMV manual and fight you for it. "Whited sepulchers," was the term Jesus used for those who loved the letter of the law more than other people. He also said, "The Sabbath was made for man, not man for the Sabbath," to those who criticized infractions of the law by the disciples. I'm afraid there'll be a lot of whining Pharisees on Judgment Day, saying, "But I kept all the rules!" The question I fear is, "Why?"

"Woe to you, teachers of the law and Pharisees, you hypocrites! You are like whitewashed tombs, which look beautiful on the outside but on the inside are full of dead men's bones and everything unclean."

—Matthew 23:27

PART TWO

CHECKING
THE MANUAL

OBJECTS IN THIS MIRROR

You can't depend too much on what you see in the mirror. There is a sense of accuracy, but actually everything is backwards. And backwards is a big difference!

Also, things you see may be larger, coming faster, and require a more immediate decision than you would think if you merely studied the mirror. A lane change you're considering may seem appropriate and safe until a glance over your shoulder at the real world convinces you otherwise. The mirror is one thing. Life is another.

My bathroom mirror tells me that this year's extra pounds don't show so very much. My three-year-old grandson tells me otherwise. My mirror tells me that I'm not getting older. I look just the same as I always did. My three-year-old grandson is living proof that I'm kidding myself.

My rearview mirror tells me that my reflexes are just as quick and dependable as they ever were. The occasional squeal of brakes from a driver I didn't see in the other lane gives me another point of view. It pays to get a second opinion.

One of life's delicious moments comes when you walk in the door and realize you're the only one home. There is no immediate work to be done. The phone, the refrigerator, the television — all the resources are yours to command. And all the judgments about how things are going are yours to make. I did just great today! I declare this day a success! Who's going to argue?

But who's going to tell you if your slip shows or that you forgot to pick up the cleaning or there's spinach in your teeth? Who's going to remind you of promises made, obligations undertaken? Who's going to nag, pester, honk, point out, argue, disagree, suggest, and proffer unwanted and contrary suggestions? Who's going to keep you between the lines?

Annoying as it is, the mirror alone can never take the place of other drivers sharing the road and helping you remember where you belong.

Woe to those who are wise in their own eyes...

—*Isaiah 5:21*

LET YOUR LIGHT SO SHINE

You don't usually know that you're doing it —
following another driver with your bright lights on
— until the driver up front shows some sign of dis-
comfort, adjusts his rearview mirror, and pulls over
to let you pass. An oncoming driver can blink his
headlights in annoyance. You realize then that

you've been bright when dim was called for.

I have a dear friend who hadn't called in quite a while. When I finally heard from her, I asked where she had been. "I've been really depressed," she told me, "and the last thing I wanted was to be around happy people."

I remembered then the days when I was preoccupied with one of my adolescent children: gloomy music, dark clothes, lack of achievement. I was afraid my child was ruined. Friends' Christmas letters listing graduations, awards, and scholarships were no pleasure to me. I sought the comforting presence of those whose kids were in really bad shape — doing drugs, maybe. In jail would be good.

If your life was falling to pieces, you were just the person I wanted to see. I didn't seek an example of courage and strength. I wanted my friends to be in terrible condition. If I was eating my way through the experience, I wanted to stand next to those who were fatter than I. The welfare of my acquaintances was not a priority. I was no fun. Because my own light was flickering, I couldn't bear the radiance of the bright ones. The night was dark, the road was long, and I wanted all the lights around me dimmed.

I had a dear friend whose life, to me, looked like a "Good Housekeeping" cover, who managed to keep a quiet, gentle light shining in my direction through those desperate days. Hers was not a bragging searchlight celebrating her success and pointing out my problems. She had no judgmental flashlight to show a better path, just a muted beam of real love, faith in me, and encouragement.

Once during my bleak days, I had been near tears as a member of our congregation explained how her solid family, her nutritious breakfasts, and her nightly educational discussions around the dinner table had propelled all of their children through college and into great marriages and careers. My friend's smirk and her rolled eyes were rude, but they saved my feelings and help me toward recovery.

So I knew what to do now for my depressed friend. I sat down beside her and said, "I know what we can do! Let's have lunch. Have you heard about creative whining?"

...pity the man who falls and has no one to help him up!

—*Ecclesiastes 4:10*

LICENSE

License: 1. freedom of action; 2. a document granted by a recognized authority to engage in specified activities; 3. a freedom that allows for irresponsibility.

It's a great feeling to have a license in your wallet. The state has declared you competent. It's legal for you to drive wherever you choose, go wherever your want. Almost. Last week, a visitor to the U.S.

was killed in his rented automobile. He had forgotten that the right lane is the one to use in the United States. Fearlessly, he had roared down the wrong lane to his death. On the same day, in my hometown, I saw a terrified, trembling woman pull over to the curb. She had turned into a one-way street and narrowly avoided a head-on collision. She wasn't hurt, but she was really scared.

My father was sixty years old and a cautious driver when a young motorcyclist tried to speed around him one night instead of waiting for Dad to execute a left turn. The boy collided with the side of my father's pickup and sent himself hurtling through a nearby fence. He had not been scared to try an illegal maneuver, and as a result, his bones were broken. My father was not hurt, but when he arrived home, weary and shaken, he said, "I never want to drive again!" He was badly frightened, but he lived to drive for many more years.

For several years in succession, some of the high school seniors in our community died on graduation night. Each was killed in the same way and by the power of the same forces: alcohol-impaired judgment and excessive speed. No graduating class seemed to have learned enough from the experience of those who had gone before to avoid meeting the same fate on the same road on the same June night. Their perception of their own invincibility and uniqueness made them heartbreakingly vulnerable. Their lack of fear destroyed them.

The average driver makes a potentially dangerous mistake once for every six minutes of driving time. Most often, there is no bad result — no collision, no ticket, no adrenaline overload. No one ever finds out. Occasionally, you may scare yourself. Rarely, you may scare another driver. If the results of the error are serious enough to foreclose your freedom of action, it only happens once.

Recently, a young friend of mine said, "When I see accidents on the road, I think, 'How can any of us drive? How is anybody brave enough to even try it?'"

It would be terrible to go down the road always frightened, but it can be deadly to underestimate the dangers that come to us with a driver's license — or to overestimate the freedom that license offers.

"The fear of the Lord is the beginning of wisdom..."

—*Proverbs 9:10*

DIRTY WINDSHIELD

There was a time when my city was well cared for. You wouldn't believe it now, to look at the junk and litter everywhere. There was a time when the schools were beautiful, with manicured lawns like parks. I can remember when someone who left a torn-down junker car in their front yard would have been fined. The whole place is going south in a handbasket. Look at those campaign signs on every pole and fence. The election was over two months ago. Look at the knocked-out letters on the movie marquee.

And these kids! There's no way you can tell me that's fashion. That's the absolute opposite of fashion. Torn, dirty, colorless. It's no wonder they can't think well! Look how they dress! The schools should go back to uniforms.

Oh, man! Tattoos! Can you believe it? Decent, respectable people are covering themselves with dark, ugly, probably Satanic symbols. It's like everyone is aspiring to look as vulgar and sleazy as possible.

Whatever happened to good manners? When did simple courtesy become obsolete? Would it kill anyone to say please or thank you once in a while?

Do you know there are countries in the world where people smile at one another just because they're members of the same species meeting on the same street? What does it cost? A smile once in a while... Some of these people look like a smile would break their faces.

And the clerks in stores! They act like they're being imposed upon just to have to help you find something or ring up your order. If you need any special help, you can expect a sigh and a big, disgruntled frown. Where's that, "My pleasure to serve you" attitude? Whatever happened to "The customer is always right," or "Give them what they want"?

It isn't like anyone in the so-called "service

industries" cares to give service anymore. It isn't like our elected representatives care what we think. It isn't like anyone anywhere can remember the basic, common courtesies that make civil life endurable. It isn't like anyone cares to keep the community a clean, pleasant place to live these days. If evolution isn't going forward, what's the point? I mean, can you point out even one area in which life is really improving? Maybe I'm a grouch, but...

All the days of the oppressed are wretched, but the cheerful heart has a continual feast.

—*Proverbs 15:15*

13

SETTING UP THE IDLE

It was just a bump on the rear end. I didn't even stop to exchange insurance information with the fellow who ran into me. There was no damage, and we just waved each other on. But I soon discovered that the idle in my VW bug had been bumped up. I was driving faster than I intended to, revving the motor at stoplights, unable to slow down. By the time I got home to see my mechanic, I was exhausted. It was hard to hold the car in line. I took my foot off the accelerator, but I accelerated anyway. I had to sit up straighter, watch traffic more intently, shift more often, change lanes constantly. The whole game was suddenly being played at fever pitch. I couldn't slow down. Climbing out of the car, my neck and shoulders ached. I felt like I'd been on a runaway horse.

James E. Loehr, author of *Toughness Training for Sports,* is a tennis coach. Studying ways to improve his players' performance, he made careful observation of how they played. He was astonished to notice that while the ball was in play, there is negligible difference between the performance of the top contenders and average players. The critical difference showed itself between points.

Between the time a tennis point is made and the ball is served again, there is approximately twenty-five seconds. Champion players use that down time to realign themselves physically and mentally for the next play. Less successful players continue whatever behavior pattern has been established by the last play. If they are angry, they exhibit angry behavior. If they have done well, they may exult, do a small victory dance. If they are disappointed, they drag themselves back to position. Good contenders waste no time on such exhibitions of emotion. They prepare for the next point in a calm, ritualistic fashion, thinking ahead. They rest.

Sometimes it feels as though our whole culture has set up its idle; there is no rest. The fact that God thought it important enough to include it in the Ten Commandments doesn't seem to help the majority of us to take that vital Sabbath recovery time. But Monday depends on Sunday. A good ride depends on setting our idle back down to where we can drive comfortably.

> *...those who hope in the Lord will renew their strength.*

—*Isaiah 40:31*

THE SAFETY ZONE

The California drivers' manual advises you to maintain a certain area around your car — an established distance between your vehicle and everyone else on the road. If they unexpectedly stop, veer, or speed up, you won't collide. You have a safety zone around you, and another person's wreck may grieve or alarm you, but it won't destroy your own vehicle.

Watching television news the other day, I longed for a safety zone. I don't want to know all this stuff. I want desperately for most of it not to be happening. But how can any of us stay out of the wrecks we see around us? How can we stay close enough to help when possible, but far enough away to keep ourselves safe?

I read once that patience protects from vexation just as a warm coat protects from the cold. Surely patience is a critical factor in maintaining a safety zone. Drivers who lose patience are a threat to those around them: vengeful, angry, aggressively seeking to move themselves forward at the expense of others on the same road. Those who become patient are willing to let other drivers choose their own course and move forward at their own speed.

Once a week, there is a different sheen to the sunlight coming in my window. The work of the week is put down and forgotten. The troubles remain, but there is a distance from them. They won't be addressed until Monday. I am looking through the closet for my best clothes. I have a vision of myself as an important daughter of God, an honored participant in the ancient tradition of the Sabbath. Sunday creates a safety zone around each of us. As we enter the well-worn pews, put flowers on the table, take time to make dessert, we are graced.

Nearly every day I have a conversation with Johann Sebastian Bach. I play a fugue, I listen to one, and suddenly my mind becomes a place of order. I am transformed by his contribution to the world.

The music creates a safe place around me and within me.

I pick up my battered Bible, and I am not helpless in the face of life's dangers. I have a manual. I know the rules. I am in a safety zone.

You will go out in joy and be led forth in peace...

—Isaiah 55:12

SPEED LIMITS

Speed limits are posted everywhere, included in driving manuals, and backed by all the authority of the state. But nobody likes them very much. If you want to understand peer pressure, to feel the full weight of public disapproval, all you have to do is pull into the fast lane and obey the speed limit. Instant unpopularity. You can actually get a ticket for obeying the limit in that situation.

But if you don't use the law to decide how fast you will travel, how do you decide? If you keep pace with everyone around you, will you be safe? A highway patrolman recently stopped my son-in-law, who had been keeping up with a group of cars. Understandably upset, he complained to the cop, "You didn't stop any of them! Just me!"

The patrolman calmly replied, "Yeah. We can do that."

It seems that no other person's behavior is much of an excuse on the day that your own is on the radar. Other drivers can lead you into trouble.

The problem is, our internal regulators don't always function, either. My car had a broken speedometer when a policeman began following me. My young daughter said, "Mom, that cop is following you!"

I smugly replied, "Don't worry, sweetie. He's not following us. I'm sure I'm not speeding. I've never had a ticket in my life!"

She said, "Mom, he turned his red light on."

I said, "Uh-oh. He must be after someone. I'll pull over so he can get around me."

I was genuinely surprised when the patrol car pulled over right behind me. Chagrined, I learned that I could be fifteen miles over the speed limit and feel just fine about it. Like the patrolman that stopped my son-in-law, this one was unimpressed with my excuse: I was doing the best I could with a broken speedometer. He seemed to believe that it was my responsibility to keep my vehicle in working order.

No one likes speed limits much, but the road would be more dangerous without them. You can't trust those around you all the time, and sometimes you can't even trust yourself. It doesn't feel like a favor when someone pulls you over to tell you that you're doing something wrong, but that message might be important — even lifesaving. There are tougher ways to learn.

Of course, there are easier ways, too. We could obey the speed limits.

He who ignores discipline despises himself...

—Proverbs 15:32

ASKING FOR DIRECTIONS

It isn't just men who hate to do it. There's a stubborn feeling that in just a minute we're going to pass the road sign we've been looking for, and then we'll never have to admit we were lost in the first place.

This is close to the right way. We're not far off the track. It feels more or less right. I have a great sense of direction, and I can sort of tell. No use to stop and ask, because it'll be embarrassing to discover how close we are. We're already there. Or at least we're almost there. I know it looks something like this. The visuals are all in place.

All right. Just a minute. If we don't see it in a couple of minutes, I'll stop and ask. I really will. Honest. But I have the feeling that we're almost there. I want to do it on my own. I want to know and prove that I can do it on my own. I don't need any help.

Asking for directions feels like cheating, for some reason. Part of the game is being able to find your way unassisted, relying only on your own resources. Asking for help is an admission of defeat, a confession of weakness, a way of saying, "I'm powerless at this moment, in this situation."

Some of us have to wander a long time before fatigue and despair humble us enough to make us ask for help. Others are humble in the first place, accept as a practical fact that no one can be expected to know a road he or she hasn't traveled before, and are quick to ask for help. Either way, the moment of humility, when we stop the car to seek guidance, brings relief.

And what a relief it is! The gratified smiles of those who were waiting, honored to be able to help, the instant clarity of the decisions before us, the easiness of the way. Suddenly it's all so simple. Why didn't I ask earlier? I could have saved myself so much time and frustration!

Next time I will. Next time I won't blunder forward when I don't know where I'm going. Next time I won't drive aimlessly, wasting energy. Next time I won't be too proud to stop and go back. Next time I'll admit my weakness. Next time I'll ask for help. Next time.

Oh, that their hearts would be inclined to fear me and keep all my commands always, so that it might go well with them and their children forever!

—Deuteronomy 5:29

READING THE MAP

They say that women are more likely than men to turn a map around and around in their hands when playing navigator. The little N arrow on the map needs to point to actual North if the map is going to make sense; it needs to be grounded in relation to the real world. The line on the paper must go in the same direction as the road I see in front of me if I am going to be able to use this map.

In the same way, any idea that is an abstract philosophical construct, like "Truth" or "Justice," must have its referent in the solid, sensory world for people to believe in its existence. A person who has never felt love will probably not be able to grasp the concept by simply reading about it. If I do not live by the principle of honesty, I will not believe that anyone I meet is honest, either.

The order and harmony that come into our world through noble concepts exist only because someone created those maps and explained them persuasively enough that the rest of us believe there is such a thing as "Liberty" or "Beauty." We believe:

"...all men are created equal, and that they are endowed by their creator with certain unalienable rights, that among these are life, liberty, and the pursuit of happiness..."

We believe this because the paper that held the words was so powerful that many of those who read it agreed to use it as a map to guide them through the world of experience.

While the trees and fields we see around us will continue to exist whether we believe in them or not, concepts like "Kindness," "Fairness," and "Honesty" will disappear forever on the day the last human being ceases to think of them. Without the map of soul-freeing principles, the world is a trackless, confusing place, where any road is as good as another.

A college girl I know returned home angry and

frustrated from a road trip where she had repeatedly gotten lost and gone miles out of her way. Asked why she hadn't used the map, she replied that she hadn't wanted to "waste time" reading it.

Not long ago, Boston citizens were surveyed about theories in the Constitution, particularly the Bill of Rights. A majority said the ideas sounded foreign, probably Communist. It would be impossible to vote according to democratic principles if one had no idea what they were and couldn't recognize them in the real world of experience.

The latitude and longitude lines that someone drew on the globe aren't real. But because we all agree to recognize them, they keep our world organized. If my plane goes down, the helicopters will use those lines to find me. If your boat sinks, you can radio your position, and because we all recognize that map, we know where to send the Coast Guard.

A map that does not correspond to external reality is useless. But without a good map, reality is just a jungle.

Recently, a young girl I know faced a situation where she had a great deal to lose if she chose to be honest. I said to her, "You've got a Daniel-in-the-lion's-den situation on your hands!" Bewildered, she said, "What's that?" There's a Bible in her house, but it's still nice and clean. All the gold on the edges of the pages is still there.

If we hope to avoid painful and costly side trips on roads we never wanted to see, we'd better spend some time with a map!

Trust in the Lord with all your heart and lean not on your own understanding; in all your ways acknowledge him, and he will make your paths straight.

—Proverbs 3:5, 6

STAYING OUT OF THE WAY

You can share the road with anyone if you can come to understand where they want to go and how to stay out of their way. Crashes come when you misunderstand someone's intentions and come between them and their objectives.

At seventy, my mother's most sincere objective is to not be trouble to anyone. If you pick up her dishes or go into the closet to find her an afghan, acts performed with kind intentions, she does not take it kindly. She growls and fusses. Her desire for autonomy is being infringed upon, and she resents the implication that she can't care for herself. You're standing between her and her goal of independence.

At nineteen, my daughter's deepest wish is also for personal autonomy. She wants to be independent, but she isn't — quite. She still needs money once in a while, some advice, someone to help iron a blouse in a hurry and hand it to her, warm, as she flies out the door. She's not glad that she needs these things, but she does. If someone provides them for her, she does not take it kindly. She growls and fusses. She resents the implication that she can't take care of herself. Nothing personal. You're just standing between her and her objective. You may feel like you're helping, but you're actually in the way.

In cases like these, support needs to be dropped, anonymously, on the doorstep, the way the cat leaves a dead gopher and doesn't stay to claim the credit. Both my mother and daughter seem to say, "You can love me; just don't make a big deal out of it. I can take care of myself." That last part is important. An expression of confidence in their ability is worth more to either of them than all the help in the world. It's the same when government provides support services to people because it doesn't believe them capable of caring for themselves. The message implicit in that action can be damaging, and that damage can outweigh the good that is done.

Sometimes I see young people in fast cars weaving in and out of traffic, choosing a lane then chang-ing their minds, speeding up, braking suddenly, erratic in their behavior, restless in their indecision. Experience has taught me a few things and I want to give advice. But these young drivers don't need advice — they need experience. There's only one thing I can do to help them. I can stay out of the way.

Therefore let us stop passing judgment on one another. Instead, make up your mind not to put any stumbling block or obstacle in your brother's way.

—Romans 14:13

PART THREE

LOOKING OUT
THE WINDOW

STUCK IN LINE

I was in a hurry. Maybe that doesn't need to be said; maybe that's a given. Sometimes it's hard to even imagine a situation in which we aren't in a hurry — anxious to get where we're going, anxious to finish what we're working on, anxious to get done, get through, get finished, get home, get it all over with.

I was the third car in the left-turn lane when it became apparent that our light wasn't going to change. The east-west drivers had gone, then the north-south drivers, then the east-west drivers again. Our left-turn arrow was not coming up on the turn signal. We were stuck.

If I had been first in line, I probably would have watched for a clear space in the traffic and overridden the light to go ahead. But I was not first in line. There was heavy traffic on both sides, going in both directions. I was trapped, and I began to feel trapped.

I started muttering, turning around to estimate my chances of getting out of this spot, tapping my foot nervously, hoping against hope that the green arrow was coming. Another round of drivers went by.

Then I noticed the young man in the junky old car in front of me. He was in the same situation, but he was responding differently. He shrugged his shoulders like, "Oh, well. There's nothing I can do about this!" Which, of course, was true.

He rolled down the window to get the sunshine on his arm. He pushed up his shirtsleeve to feel that sunshine better. He fiddled with the dial on his radio until he found a song that suited him. He began to dance, right there, sitting in his car in the middle of a traffic tie-up. Just a little swaying motion at first, but soon the music got him. He turned it up.

There are only so many really good dance moves that a person can develop sitting down. This guy seemed to be trying to find them all. He paid no attention to what anyone observing him might think. He was having a wonderful time.

Eventually, the light decided to change and we were released from the turn lane. We went our various ways, most of us annoyed and frustrated by the delay. One of us went ahead refreshed and happier because of the unexpected intermission. But, of course, he brought his own music.

Sing to the Lord, all the earth...

—*I Chronicles 16:23*

BROWNIAN MOTION AND MEXICAN TAXI DRIVERS

Mexican city traffic is a visual physics lesson. In physics, Brownian motion is explained as the haphazard trembling of matter caused by random molecular collisions. You don't need a microscope to see an example. It's a phenomenon that can be observed in any Mexican city during rush hour traffic —

which, in some cases, lasts approximately all day. The more time you spend on the road there, the more likely you are to find yourself trembling in a haphazard way.

I understood the rules of play a little better after I went along on a driving lesson one day. My hostess was teaching her niece, who had already mastered the mechanics of starting, stopping, and shifting, how to get around in city traffic.

We went into the *centro* for the lesson, and the girl was obviously terrified. I could tell by the steady, quiet scream coming from the back of her throat the whole time. I was more than a little bit frightened myself. My hostess turned up the music and picked up her knitting.

"First rule, *mi hija*. Ignore the stop signs. If you obey them, you will surprise the person behind you, and they will ram into you from the back."

"But what about the drivers coming in from the sides?"

"Don't look at them. If they think you see them, they will expect you to stop for them. Look straight ahead and pretend you don't see anyone else."

By this time, I was trying to suppress the scream in my own throat. I estimated my chances of jumping out at the next stop, but under these rules it didn't seem that there would be a next stop.

There were cars straddling the center line, six or seven abreast where there was room, then the imaginary lanes suddenly disappearing to allow room for only one or two cars beside each other, horns honking, speed limits set by the individual and his or her personal goals: it was a thrilling ride. When we pulled up to the house, it was all I could do to keep from throwing myself on the ground to kiss the sidewalk.

Later, leaving the city, I had a chance to ask an experienced taxi driver how he remained calm in such apparent chaos. I had been surprised to observe no anger on the crowded, confused streets. When people honked, it was only to notify others of their presence. When they waved, they used all their fingers. I saw no actual collisions, although the dented-in sides of cars were evidence that accidents happened on a regular basis.

I was amazed at my driver's equanimity. "Why don't you get angry?" I asked him. "Why aren't you upset?"

He seemed surprised at the question. "Look around," he instructed me. "There are too many of us here. If I got angry every time somebody made a mistake, I would be angry all the time. I don't want to live that way. What would be the use?"

Oh. I sat back in my seat, nodding. There are too many of us here to allow random collisions to upset us. What would be the use?

Better a patient man than a warrior...

—*Proverbs 16:32*

68

THE DESIGNATED DRIVER

The whole incident lasted only a few seconds. No one was hurt, exactly. But over the next several days, I thought about it again and again. I was waiting at a downtown intersection, several cars back in line. A white-haired man, peering over the top of his steering wheel, began a left turn in his shiny antique Studebaker. Midway through the turn, he seemed to get confused and stopped to read the street signs again. Traffic in both directions was held up for a minute.

The young guy in the shiny black pickup behind the Studebaker gleefully hit the gas. Just before crashing into the older man's rear end, he stomped on the brakes. The pickup fishtailed, leaving rubber in the street. Tires squealing, the young man pulled around the Studebaker and turned in front of the older man, who eventually figured out the direction he wanted and proceeded up the street.

The image that stayed with me, and seemed to be on the back of my eyelids when I tried to sleep that night, was the face of the passenger in the pickup. She was a teenage girl, apparently not belted in. The sudden stop threw her against the windshield, arms crossed in front of her face. Her expression was one of terror, which quickly changed to fury.

She was angry, not at the driver she had chosen to carry her around town, but at the old man blocking the intersection. Rolling down the window, she raised her middle finger toward the Studebaker and screamed an obscenity. She glanced at her driver, checking for his approval, but it was impossible to tell at this point whether the young man's scowl was for her or the old man. It was just a generic, "Life sucks!" kind of frown. In seconds, they disappeared up the street.

I felt a chill of terror for that girl. When you get into someone's car, you literally put your life in their hands. I wanted to roll down my window and yell to her, "Hey, girl! Get out and walk! There are lots of shiny black pickups in this world!" But, of course, she was gone.

He who walks with the wise grows wise, but a companion of fools suffers harm.

—*Proverbs 13:20*

RESPECT

(re=again; spect=look—LOOK AGAIN)

Mornings at the adult school often made me grumpy. As a teacher of English as a Second Language, I felt a responsibility to see that the whole country made a good impression on our newcomers. My students had traveled and often suffered to be in this country, and I felt that they deserved a better welcome than an obstacle course of litter and a lot of unwanted music. Rude dropouts coming back to make up high school credits and scattering their potato chip bags and beer cans were an embarrassment.

I heard the blaring heavy metal music before I saw the kids in the beat-up old car approach the curb. I was in no mood for them. A lot of effort was required to patrol the litter on campus, and I was just getting into my muttering morning routine with my books temporarily stacked on the sidewalk while I gathered garbage.

What I saw confirmed my worst suspicions. The low-rider car was dented and painted over with hippie flowers.The boy driving and his girl passenger had matching hair: long, straight, blonde, dry, and uncut. The jalopy jerked to a stop not far from where I was throwing trash into the garbage can.

I was practicing the glare I intended to give them when something unexpected caught my attention. The boy had turned off the car and was walking around to open the door for his girlfriend. I hadn't seen anyone behave like that for a long time. He reached in for the books she was carrying, and offered the other hand to help her out of the car. She smiled her thanks and stepped out as gracefully as any princess. Then she frowned.

"Baby, I'm scared. I don't think I can do this."

"Hey, you'll do great. I'll be right here after class and if you do good, I'll let you select from the 79¢ menu for lunch."

She grinned. "I love you."

"Of course you do. I'm great!"

He may have been right about that. You just never can tell. But his girlfriend and I were both smiling as he pulled out into traffic, tires squealing and gravel flying. A driver who had to brake for him frowned and shook his fist. I was appalled at that attitude. As I picked up my books, I was muttering to myself again: "What an old buzzard! How can some people be so quick to judge and so slow to try to understand?"

"Man looks at the outward appearance, but the Lord looks at the heart."

—*I Samuel 16:7*

MY VERY FIRST ACCIDENT

Rushing into a nearby house, I yelled to my young daughter to do what she could for the victim of the bicycle accident while I called 911. When I came back outside, I was astonished to see that she hadn't moved the bicycle off the road, picked up the fallen girl's schoolbooks, which were scattered everywhere, or even asked her if anything was broken.

My daughter was staring at the child with fascination, not two feet from her face, as if the girl were an inanimate object. She was obviously enthralled by this new circumstance, oblivious to the other girl's feelings. She said to me with excitement, "Mom! This is my very first accident!" As it turned out, the child had not been seriously hurt, but when the ambulance came, I saw my daughter glancing toward our car, where her camera was in the glove compartment. I know she wanted to take a picture with herself in it.

There's no way to point out to a ten- or twelve-year-old that all life's events don't belong exclusively to them. The rest of us on the planet are just scenery. It's their play, and they have all the lines. It's difficult for them to even imagine other people's feelings.

Hopefully, as we mature, we come to realize that the accidents — or the days, or the parties, or the Christmas mornings — belong to other people, too. It's an index of maturity, I think, when a young person shows up to applaud someone else's show, weep at someone else's funeral, form part of the crowd at someone else's wedding.

This same daughter took me to a concert last week. I had lots of things to do, but I was trying to be courteous and enjoy it for her sake, when I heard her whisper to her own little girl, "You have to be good so Grandma can enjoy her music. She needs a rest."

These days she's always got a camera with her, but she's never in the pictures. She's always cooking someone else's favorite dish. I suppose, in her own mind, she's moved into the scenery. In my mind, she's just begun to really shine.

"Many women do noble things, but you surpass them all."

—*Proverbs 31:29*

TALKING YOUR WAY THROUGH

"Whoops! Shouldn't have tried to get in there!"

"Yikes! I'd better speed up if I'm going to merge."

"Now look what he's done. Where am I supposed to go?"

"Sorry about that, mister."

"Watch where you're going, lady!"

My daughter's freeway experience is an endless stream of chatter. And all those words are important, though no other driver ever hears them. They define and clarify for her what's happening. Without words, life is just a parade of unrelated images, rushing past in a meaningless stream. Like MTV. Without the words, there's no way to sort one's own experiences.

When this same daughter was a teenager, she used to get angry on a regular basis. She never mentioned it, but I knew about it by the way she stomped to her room, slammed the door, and reached under her bed for her journal. The pen would fly across the page for a while — sometimes a long while — until she figured out how she felt and took a position. She often accused me of reading that journal, but of course I never did. That was the last thing I wanted to read! All the anger in those pages might have vaporized me on the spot. The journal served the important purpose of containing that hostility, making it safe for both of us.

I remember Mary Ellen Ferguson. When I was eight years old, Mary Ellen Ferguson punched me in the stomach on the day I brought a live bat I had found to Brownies, making it simultaneously the best and worst day of my whole life so far.

Rushing to my side, the Brownie leader asked how I felt. Was I okay? I wasn't sure. I was definitely feeling some things, but I had no idea what they were. I nodded and she let me go home, frowning mightily at Mary Ellen Ferguson.

"Oh, Mom!" I ran breathlessly in the door. My

mother sat back on the couch, braced for the daily assault of words. "You won't believe it! It was so... *embarrassing!*" Oh. Now I knew. I instantly felt better. Sometimes, one word is worth a thousand pictures.

...and how good is a timely word!

—Proverbs 15:23

IT'S ON FIRE! IT'S MY CAR!

I had never seen a person so completely double-minded. When smoke began pouring out from under the hood of his car, he jumped out and took off running. Half a block away, he turned and ran back just as fast.

Considering the real possibility of an imminent explosion, he about-faced again and ran away. But his steps got slower, and soon he reversed himself one more time.

What to do? He was unarmed against a fire, but unwilling to abandon his car. Back and forth he ran at top speed — unable to stay, unable to leave. Since that day, I've seen many people in similar situations: jobs or families in disrepair — agonies of decision where no choice looks good. Back and forth. And back. And forth.

One of the most painful of such crises comes when a loved child matures into a person of poor judgment or values, someone with whom you would never choose to associate if he or she weren't your family, someone you might even cross the street to avoid if he or she weren't related to you. The situation is often remarkably similar:

"He's a tattooed, motorcycle-riding, gun-carrying, neo-Nazi white supremacist. But he's my son!"

"She's a lying, cheating, stealing, immoral drug dealer. But she's my daughter!"

Which way do you run? Toward or away from?

A wise man once said, "Pray that we will have the courage never to desert our children in some dark and dangerous thoroughfare of life — no matter how they came to be there."

You can never know when the right word or touch from you might have power to put out the fires of rage and self-hatred. I remember a summer evening years ago when I stared into the screaming, mascara-streaked face of my beloved teenage daughter. Waves of flaming anger poured from her, palpable in the air. She was unrecognizable to me. I actually thought, "Who *is* this person? What happened to my daughter?"

I had no weapon against such a conflagration except the enormous love God grants to parents. I had never loved her as deeply as I did in that moment. It was enough.

"A new command I give you: Love one another."

—*John 13:34*

THE GIFT

I'm not going to say it happens every time. But I've seen it more than occasionally. My friend Dale, a good guy, worked overtime shifts for months with one objective: he planned to surprise his only daughter with a new car for graduation.

After the wreck, when the mangled car was

being hauled out of the ditch and his tearful daughter was apologizing for the tenth time, he mentioned that he had felt funny about the project all along — some kind of premonition that it wasn't the best idea in the world. But he wanted to be a good dad. More than a good dad — a great dad!

Another man I know bought a gorgeous sports car for himself. There was no room for anyone in the family to ride along, which was the whole idea. But somewhere inside, deeply buried, was the certain knowledge that, sooner or later, one of them would wheedle him in a weak moment, and he would break his cardinal rule: nobody drives this car but me.

The moment came on prom night: an important girlfriend to impress, a desperate seventeen-year-old son. He wanted to be a great father. All right. Just this once. Another ditch — actually, more like a cliff this time. Another shaken, sorry teenager. Another car destroyed.

I saw similarities this week as I cried a few tears with a saddened mother. "I wanted to give my children religion as a gift. I took them to church every Sunday from the time they were tiny, hoping they would love it as I do. They've gone to church all their lives, and I still make them go, but they can't wait to get away from it."

There's a kid in our town who drives around in a beat-up old Oldsmobile, a gas hog and a public eyesore. Every door is a different color; the hood, trunk and hubcaps are decorated with hand-painted hippie designs. It's a worthless hunk of junk, but he doesn't seem to notice. In fact, he celebrates his car.

He changes the paintings every few days, drives with the windows down and the radio up, smiles at oncoming traffic. I see him sometimes in his driveway, checking the oil or the air pressure in the tires. I believe that many years from now, remembering that car, he will smile. Nobody gave it to him. He put it together all by himself.

> *...choose for yourselves this day whom you will serve...*

—*Joshua 24:15*

NERVOUS IN THE CHOIR

She was beautiful Sunday in her white blouse, singing heavenly music in the chorus of the saints. But she kept wringing her hands, dabbing an occasional tear with her handkerchief, smoothing its crocheted edges into squares on her lap. What use is a gorgeous Sabbath morning when your children are God knows where, doing God knows what?

Her kids were unusually prone to car accidents; she never really slept well until they were all in the house at night. She was safe on the freeway, but they were not. There is no place on earth pleasant enough, secure enough, heavenly enough, to be happy there while loved ones are wandering about in risky places.

Watching her, I learned what angels do with their time: they worry about everyone else. They cook great dinners to lure us to stay in the safe havens of home. They wear elegant clothes to make virtue attractive. They decorate houses and fill them with music and flowers and the smell of chocolate chip cookies.

They dispense smiles and money and compliments, new clothes for our new beginnings, and suggestions full of hope. They take our pictures and paste them in books. They clap a lot, and yell at referees who don't see things our way. They rejoice — and finally relax — only when we prove to them that we are able to find our own way down the road.

Until that day, they may be singing sacred music in a sunlit choir loft, but their hearts are with us sharing the perils of the highway. Often we're not aware of their presence, preoccupied as we are with our gauges and dials, piloting our own vehicles with ferocious independence.

A young friend of mine credits his mother with the strength he mustered to leave a street gang that had held him for several years. "I hated her for a long time, because she wouldn't let me go. She was with me everywhere I went. When I finally came to myself, she was still there. Thank God!"

Turns out harp-playing and hymn-singing is harder work than it looks. And it matters more, too. Some people say you can't save the world. They're wrong. I know sopranos and altos who are doing it every day.

She watches over the affairs of her household... Her children arise and call her blessed...

—*Proverbs 31:27, 28*

OUT OF GAS

How could a person not know he is almost out of gas? For a while, it was a joke in our family, carrying gas cans to one of us who was forever stranded beside the road. We all wondered why he chose to live his life in that little area between 1/8 and E. But we each do the same thing in different ways.

Children do it most noticeably. My tiny grand-daughter, exhausted to the point of screaming crankiness, will not slow down. "You're tired, sweet-ie. You need a rest."

Her last ounce of strength goes into the defiant response, "NO!"

There's something in a two-year-old's view of the world that makes it important not to accept a fill-up when one is needed. Grumpy, desperate for the assurance of a hug, they squirm away. Hungry for a nourishing meal, they refuse to eat. If they are really tired, they avoid sleep, fighting to keep their eyes open, anxious to prove themselves inex-haustible.

Teenagers scowl at their parents, determined to prove them wrong. Wrong about everything. They don't need a curfew, or breakfast, or any rules. They are just fine, thank you. What they need is less inter-ference and more freedom. If everyone would just leave them alone, and let them borrow another ten dollars until the end of the week, and have the car, they could manage themselves perfectly well.

A parent's strongest stance is that of filling sta-tion. Sooner or later, everyone has to come to the parent for basic physical and emotional needs. Meeting those needs consistently and kindly will create a safe atmosphere, in which a person may ultimately find the courage to admit vulnerabilities.

My tiny granddaughter is growing up. She will live through the defiant two-year-old scramble for independence. I know she will be three soon. I can feel it coming on. Just yesterday she said to me, "Meemaw, I'm tired. I need a rest!"

And a few weeks ago our darling boy surrendered his defiance of the laws of physics and filled up the tank. Life goes on.

And we urge you... be patient with everyone.

—*I Thessalonians 5:14*

INTO THE COW PASTURE

When my young visitor finally convinced me that he was serious, that he was happy about the dragon tattoo on his shoulder and determined to pierce his belly button, along with several other sensitive areas, I asked him why. Was this a rite of manhood, a demonstration of courage? Was he accepting and symbolically submitting himself to the inevitable pain of life on this earth? What was his philosophical position? Where was the symbolism? What did he mean by this behavior?

I was prepared for almost any metaphor, but not for the answer he actually gave: "I just think it looks cool, and I like to shock people."

It was like an experience some friends of mine had driving in a strange state on a very foggy night. Unable to see the line that would have kept them on the road, unable to feel the built-in bumps that let you know when you're leaving your lane, they were without direction in a strange gray world. They made very little progress and had to move very slowly, with no way to gauge if they were getting where they hoped to go.

As it turned out, my friends were leaders in a line of traffic. They didn't know about the other cars, either. They were so cut off from the world by the thick fog that they were unable to see anyone ahead, and were unaware of anyone behind. When you're thoroughly lost, everything around you looks the same. Differences between one thing and another are blurred.

After what seemed a long time of wandering without direction, a turn-off presented itself and they took it, hoping for a clearer course. Within a few minutes, they discovered themselves in an open pasture, surrounded by fields of manure. Worse, several of the drivers behind them had followed, just because their taillights had been the most clearly visible directors on the road.

To be a leader in a dark time, it doesn't seem to

be necessary to know where you're going. If your light is the only one people can see, you can lead those coming behind off the road and into a pile of manure. I read recently that another piercing parlor has opened in our community offering various ceremonies of self-mutilation. My young acquaintance was without purpose or direction, but others are following him anyway.

Those who guide this people mislead them...

—Isaiah 9:16

SHARING THE ROAD

JUST LIKE A CADILLAC

I'm not prejudiced. Certainly not. Far from it. But when was the last time you saw a Cadillac slow down for someone? Have you ever seen a BMW obey the speed limit? It just doesn't happen. Certain kinds of people buy certain kinds of cars, and those kinds of people have certain behavior patterns. Why do you think highway patrolmen keep such a close watch on red cars and convertibles? That's not prejudice. It's a simple fact of life.

And the other day a Cadillac — naturally — pulled right out in front of me in heavy traffic. The driver didn't seem to care whether any other cars might be inconvenienced by this course of action, or even whether other cars existed. Those Cadillac people are just not like the rest of us. They feel entitled to their own separate laws, which have nothing to do with the normal give and take of sharing the road.

I was incensed enough to speed up and try to pull around the car — if for no other reason than to notify the driver that there really were others of us on the street. As I pulled into the second lane and glared, I was taken aback to see a familiar face smiling at me. My friend! The situation was instantly clear: this good person had not seen me or the other cars. She had unknowingly endangered herself pulling into traffic. She could have been killed. Thank goodness she was all right!

Just a face. A familiar face, one that I'd seen before and come to trust. But the sight of the face inside the car completely reversed my interpretation of events. That's how all prejudice in the world is overcome — one face at a time.

"Stop judging by mere appearances, and make a right judgment."

—*John 7:24*

THE CARPOOL LANE

If you're going to use a much-traveled road during a much-traveled time, take someone along. If you're going to employ thousands of pounds of machinery to get you to work, take someone along. That's the position of the California Department of Transportation. They reward those who carpool with faster transit across bridges, reduced tolls, better parking spaces.

Still, most cars on today's freeways have seating space for five, but have only one person inside. Coworkers on the same shift pull up beside each other, parking individual cars in individual parking places. Sometimes we justify to ourselves and each other that riding together wouldn't work; there are a lot of errands to take care of on the way home and schedules are irregular.

Before we took to microwaving individual "Lean Cuisines" and calling it dinner, there was always room for one more at the table. If you cooked enough for two, there was enough for three. If you cooked enough for four, you could feed five. It was sort of a law. Now, we all wander through the same house, but we select different entrees and eat on different schedules. I can eat exactly what I want. There's no need to agree with anyone, no cooperative process to go through. There are no leftovers for you.

Most houses have a couch that makes into a bed or even an extra bedroom. But in recent years, responding to calls for homes where an exchange student or traveling dancers with a university troupe could be put up, no one thinks they have room.

"We're never here."

"I couldn't guarantee to provide transportation; I've got a really busy schedule."

"It would be terrible for someone to stay at my house. I'm gone all the time."

"We couldn't provide meals. We just don't sit down to dinner anymore. We eat out all the time."

Carpooling is stress. People have annoying habits. They never seem to want to go exactly where you do at exactly the same time. But when the sunset is beautiful, or the dinner is delicious, or the traffic is terrible, or the errands are exhausting, it's a real comfort to be sitting next to someone who thinks so too. We need to get back into the carpool lane.

A man that hath friends must show himself friendly.

—*Proverbs 18:24 (KJV)*

SLOW DOWN FOR CHILDREN

It's not as though you have a choice. The presence of children makes it necessary for all adults around them to slow down. That's one of the vital purposes they serve. And they do it in a variety of ways.

"I have to go to the bathroom."

"I'm hungry."

"Are we there yet?"

Nothing is simple anymore; no journey is a straight shot. If it used to take ten minutes to get to church, it will now take thirty. And you often see young mothers who routinely come in fifteen or twenty minutes late, confused and not yet adapted to the new time requirements in their lives. Their faces say, "I left on time. What happened?"

A young school administrator I know is a first-time mother. She recently adopted a newborn, and found herself adjusting to the responsibilities of parenthood in a very sudden way. Visiting her in the office the other day, I asked her how the process was going. She replied that there was good news and bad news.

"The bad news is that I can't get as much work done." She proved her point by jumping up in answer to a cry from the playpen behind her desk. Carrying back baby, bottle, and blanket, she smiled at me. "The good news is that I don't care. My priorities have shifted. Nothing on this desk will ever be as important to me as it was before. And that feels really good. I love my work, but I love something else more."

Another friend is among those who decided that children didn't fit into her tightly planned agenda. She and her husband would wait until they finished graduate school, wait until they had a bigger house, wait until he got the promotion, wait. Now in their late forties, it suddenly appears to them that they have been rushing at top speed for twenty years. They got educations, good jobs, nice cars, a

105

boat, several beautiful houses — each bigger than the last. They got and got, and they waited and waited. Holding her coworker's new baby the other day, tears came to this dear friend's eyes. "Nothing I have seems important to me now. If I had it to do over…" She couldn't finish the sentence. If you have the opportunity, slow down for children.

"Let the little children come to me, and do not hinder them…"

—Luke 18:16

JERICHO ROAD

I suppose it is actually no more of a risk to pick up hitchhikers on Highway 29 in the 1990s than it was for a Jew to stop on the Jericho road to help a victim of thieves two thousand years ago. But we often say that things are just too dangerous now.

It's not like it used to be, when all humanity

shared a common code of ethics and decency and a man's word was as good as his bond. In those good old days, (whenever they were), truckers would stop for you. Most people were trustworthy.

Now, the world has gone to pieces. What looks to be a scene of distress is probably a setup by vicious con men. Violence is everywhere. A person can't afford to take chances these days.

And I don't. I've driven past stranded vehicles that caused me a real pang of guilt and remorse. I feel like a Levite priest, but I keep driving. If I'm alone, I don't stop because I have no man with me. With my husband, I used to say that I didn't stop because he wouldn't permit it.

But occasionally, someone wills me to stop and I find that I must. Later, I wonder why. Why would one person's misadventure be more powerful than another's? Recently, a man looked at me from the weeds beside the road. I didn't make it 100 yards beyond his face. I applied my brakes and pulled over as automatically and fearlessly as a robot programmed to respond. Chatting with him over a gas can on the way to the closest Chevron station, I wondered what force he had exerted. Why did I stop?

Well, for one thing, he looked like me — not because his features resembled mine, but because he was about my age and my coloring, chose a style of dress that made sense to me, drove a car in my price range. He was obviously a person with whom I could identify. I felt that I could predict his behavior, and I was right. I can risk compassion for those like me.

A young couple in our community is adopting a

pair of Russian youngsters this summer. The children are six and eight years old. They don't speak English, and their new parents don't understand Russian. In fact, Cindy was showing people at work their names. "Does anyone know how to pronounce this?"

Those children are not like their adopted parents. They have little shared experience. They never met before the moment in the airport when they declared themselves an instant family. There are a million things to fear in a situation like that one. So many things could go wrong! What if those children are brain-damaged, drug-damaged, traumatized beyond saving? What if you just plain don't like them? What if they don't like you?

This young couple is undaunted by fears. They are bonded by a compassion and understanding much deeper and wider than shared ethnicity or social position. This couple feels a connection with the whole world. Similarities are not required. I think they have something to teach those of us who are too timid to offer ourselves.

Samaritans were not much like Jews, either. The animosities between the two communities were deep and often deadly. But it was a Samaritan that Jesus called "neighbor."

Which of these three do you think was a neighbor to the man...?

—*Luke 10:36*

GRIDLOCK

The whole concept is terrifying. The open road is before us, designed to let everyone travel in the direction he chooses. The state — that's us — has gone to enormous expense to provide us each with the means of smooth, safe locomotion. But now I can't move and you can't either. Pedestrians are walking faster than our high-powered cars. Bicyclists will be home before us.

If one of us goes into labor or has a heart attack — good luck! We're thrown entirely upon our individual resources, caught in a pattern none of us can break, unable to be of help to one another, furious at each other for just existing, for trying to go in the same direction at the same time, for getting in the way.

Suddenly we are not friends and fellow travelers. We are ferocious competitors for every open space, every break in the traffic. We are enemies. You are between me and my objective. I wish you weren't on my planet, taking up all the air and water, using up all the fossil fuel, getting all the good jobs. We need population control. I, of course, belong here, but the rest of you are another matter.

In times of social stress, like recessions, we look for someone to blame. Who brought this chaos upon us? Welfare mothers? Communists? Blacks? Liberals? Jews? Illegal immigrants?

In California, where many feel choked, crowded, and taxed to death, the pressure becomes particularly strong. High taxes for social services have caused many businesses to leave the state, taking jobs with them. The huge numbers of illegal immigrants fighting for a place to earn a living has created a backlash of hatred. And the hatred is breeding a new generation of angry youth.

As usual, there's only one force strong enough to break gridlock. The wandering, errant Children of Israel were given powerful instructions about this issue:

111

"When an alien lives with you in your land, do not mistreat him. The alien living with you must be treated as one of your native-born. Love him as yourself, for you were aliens in Egypt. I am the Lord your God."

—*Leviticus 19:33-34*

There's no other way to get home.

BLIND SPOTS

I know about yours. Your blind spot causes you to pull into the same lane I'm trying to get into. You aren't foolhardy or rude; you just can't see me because of the position I occupy in your field of vision. You're blind to me. Logically, I know that I have a blind spot or two of my own. Every so often, someone leaps into the corner of my eye that must have been there for a while, but this is the first I knew about it.

As a teacher, this phenomenon happens frequently with students. Focusing on a student with a particular charm or need or interest that requires attention from me, I fail to see someone else as an individual until the student with the pressing need or attention-getting personality has returned to the group. Suddenly, the next person stands out, his or her needs and interests become my focus and I am astonished that I hadn't noticed him or her before.

When our congregation split a couple of years ago along geographical lines, I was dismayed to see that everyone I liked and spent time with had gone into the other group. Walking into a full chapel, I actually thought to myself, "There's no one here!" Last week, I walked into the same chapel, saw the same faces, and thought, "Oh, good! Vacations must be over for the summer. Everyone's here!" During those two years, some wonderful people had moved out of my blind spot and into my field of vision.

I had an embarrassing experience at my twentieth high school reunion. A smiling face said, "I bet you don't remember me!" and I didn't. Turned out we had been in classes together all four years. I joked that he must have gone to the wrong junior high school. No, we had been together in seventh and eighth grade as well. It got worse. We had the same sixth grade teacher, had sat next to each other all year. "That explains it," I thought. "If he was right next to me, he was in my blind spot." When I went home to check my yearbook, the young face had no

114

familiarity, either. I had completely overlooked an entire person — and a very nice one — for seven years! He just never came to my attention.

What you're looking for may be close by. Check your blind spot.

"... first take the plank out of your own eye..."

—Matthew 7:5

SIGNALS

She was signaling that she intended to turn left. I believed her.

When I pulled out in front of her, however, I saw that she had no intention of turning. We nearly collided, and both of us lost patience. She was obviously incensed, and I was just as angry. I don't know whether she even knew that she was sending a signal. Maybe she intended to make a left turn further down the road and the signal was an early expression of future intentions. Maybe the signal was an accident, left over from an earlier change of direction. Whatever it was, I made a serious mistake by depending on it in the absence of any accompanying behavior. I would have been wiser to observe whether she slowed down, veered in the direction she indicated, or gave some other sign that she actually intended to change direction.

A friend of mine is a junior in high school. I love many qualities about him: he is fair, honest, quick to learn, and fun to be with — the kind of kid that teachers love to have in class, girls watch when he walks by, and mothers point out to their friends. He dresses like the gang members at his school: black baggy pants, white ironed T-shirt with Jesus bleeding on the back, and a net on his head. Those of us who know him don't misread that signal. His behavior has shown us that it is safe to love and trust the person underneath the giant serape that droops around his ankles. Trouble is, not everybody knows him.

Not long ago, a committee met to choose a youth representative from our area to visit Mexico at the request of President Salinas de Gortari. Based on grades, motivation and leadership qualities, Armando had been recommended by his teachers and the school counselor. The committee, however, was solemn but firm in their decision: his clothes sent the wrong signal, made the wrong impression. Someone else would spend a week in the palace in

Mexico City. Armando, of course, never knew he had been under consideration for the fabulous opportunity. He had no occasion to ponder the effects of the signals he sent on those around him and how they affected his life and future. I don't know if he would have changed his signals, but he had no chance to decide. The opportunity came and went without his knowledge.

In L.A. not long ago, a newly arrived immigrant had bought gang clothing to look like his American cousins. A cop looking for a hold-up man wearing the same clothing, asked him several times to stop, but he didn't understand the word. He was shot and killed.

If the driver I almost hit had had the chance to evaluate her signal, I don't know if she would have changed what she was doing. Maybe it was deliberate. Maybe it was not. Either way, an inaccurate signal brought us to the edge of disaster. And some people, like the little gangster in L.A., don't make it back from that edge.

Do not lie to each other...

—*Colossians 3:9*

THE GUY BEHIND ME

He's pressuring me. I don't want to go this fast, but he's right on my tail, and I certainly don't want to change lanes and get behind that beat-up old pickup. I'm irritated because I'm going faster than I want to, trying to match the pace of someone who has no right to dictate how fast I go. I could pull over, but I like that old pickup's snail crawl even less. Now I'm really speeding, but it's not my fault. I'm a victim of peer pressure, and it's making my ride uncomfortable.

Am I accountable here? Could a policeman pull me over and charge me? Would he say, as my mother often did, "If he were going over a cliff, would you go with him?" But how can I slow down with him so close behind? I can already feel his irritation. He thinks I'm holding him up.

Now I'm coming up fast on someone who's really poking along in the passing lane. Move over, fella. If you can't keep up, get out of the way. For a minute, it feels as though I may be crushed between the two of them. The slow driver pulls over at the last second. I don't follow. I don't want to travel behind him, and there's a clear space ahead.

If I can get past these few cars, I'll be able to pull over into an empty lane. I can set my own pace, choose my own speed. Just a few more hundred yards. This is going to be a big relief. There we go. Now I can relax, cut back on the Indianapolis 500 stuff, enjoy this trip.

But he's following me! He's pulled over directly behind me, reduced his speed along with me. So did the car behind him, and the car behind that. Well, if all of us are so anxious to slow down, why were we flying down the highway together at eighty miles an hour?

Here comes the answer now: a teenager in a new Neon that's already got a banged-up fender, wanting more speed, more action, more freedom —

driving the whole community in front of him, all of us trying to keep up with his pace. I hear the siren behind us before I see anything. I'm not exactly smug, but I'm grateful that I made it into the middle lane for a medium speed. There's time for every purpose under Heaven...

...*mere children will govern them. People will oppress each other — man against man, neighbor against neighbor.*

—Isaiah 3:4, 5

121

DRIVING WELL

At first, there was just a tiny, niggling sense of dread as I followed her unfamiliar car down a crowded city street. Someone in the oncoming lane was waiting to make a left turn across our lane. Though we had no stop sign, she stopped unexpectedly to let the oncoming car turn in front of us. My car, and two or three others behind me, had to brake suddenly.

Confused at the reversal of protocol, the turning driver stayed put, refusing to budge. So did we all. Standoff. That was a bother. We were stopped a full minute before someone finally broke the deadlock and we all drove on.

Although there were no stop signs or lights on the street we were traveling, she came to a full stop at each intersection. That was more than a bother. It was a worry. I slowed down, not wanting to follow her too closely and risk a rear-ender. There was no way to predict when she might stop.

But when we did come to a red light, she drove straight through without a glance toward the traffic coming in from the sides. The dread grew. I did not want to be on the road with this person. I had no way to determine what she would do next. She was driving without rules.

I knew exactly what I wanted from her. I didn't want her to be more compassionate, more careful, slower, or faster. I only wanted her to obey the rules of the road just the way they're written in the drivers' manual. I wanted to be able to depend on her behavior. Simple, predictable obedience to the law was the greatest gift she could have given her fellow drivers. Without it, no thoughtful, random courtesies could make up for its lack. Chaos surrounded her.

As soon as I could, I turned onto another road and breathed a sigh of relief. I had to wait a long time with my left-turn signal on before all the drivers going straight had gone by and it was my turn. I didn't mind.

123

"Be very strong; be careful to obey all that is written in the Book of the Law... without turning aside to the right or to the left."

—*Joshua 23:6*

KILLING WITH KINDNESS

The first step was good intentions. Seeing the harried-looking mother standing with her baby stroller in the pedestrian lane at the side of the road, the young driver felt sympathetic. Without much warning to the driver behind him, he braked abruptly to offer the woman a chance to cross the street. The driver following him was annoyed, but able to stop. No harm done.

The next step was the beginning of trouble. It was necessary to somehow indicate to the drivers in the other three lanes of traffic that they should stop, too. There was, however, no way to accomplish this. He frowned at the other drivers mightily and smiled at the young mother, vigorously waving her into the street. The driver in the next lane, oblivious to all this action and unable to see around the stopped car, hit the mother and her baby, killing both.

In an attempt to make the road a more courteous place, the young driver had actually perpetrated a disaster, and he is not free from responsibility. It's easy to say that the mother would have preferred to wait a very long time for a clear space in the traffic if she had known that the alternative was never to arrive home at all. She had trusted in the kindness of someone who had no power to create the safety he was trying to offer her. Out of deep, sympathetic feelings for old growth forests, laboratory animals, unborn babies, whales, tigers, and others who are defenseless, people are often moved to destructive acts. Destroy the bulldozers and backhoes, release the helpless animals, sink the whaling boats, bomb the abortion clinic! Such actions will show the world exactly who is compassionate and who is heartless. Condemn the beliefs and actions of those who do not agree with you, graphically and dramatically, if possible. Throw animal blood on the rich woman's new fur coat. Pitch rotten fruit at the beauty contest with its devaluation of human beings. It's not hard to demonstrate the callousness of mankind. And you can make your point even more strongly if someone gets hurt through your actions. But you have crossed a dangerous line here. You have become part of the forces of destruction and separation. Fighting for a better world, you have made things worse.

I don't suppose Christianity can make much headway in the world until we feel genuine empathy for the Nazi, the Skinhead, the Ku Klux Klan member, and all the other drivers in all the other lanes and ways of thinking.

Until we can hold the murdered baby and the abortion doctor, Hitler and the Jews, victim and victimizer in our hearts at the same time, we have no real kindness, and certainly no safety, to offer the world. Like the self-righteous young driver, we will continue to invite the innocent out into the traffic — just to prove our point.

"Beware of your friends; do not trust your brothers."

—*Jeremiah 9:4*

RUSH HOUR HARMONY

It's unexpected and thrilling when it occurs: the sudden feeling that all is as it should be, that the universe is humming along in good order. The last time it happened to me, I was driving home from the airport through the confusing maze that Oakland highways have been since the earthquake that caused so much destruction. Repairs to the freeway system have not been completed after all these years; several lanes were virtually at a standstill; my car was overheating from time to time; I was going to be late. It was an unlikely situation to feel at peace with the cosmos.

But as the sun goes down and headlights come on, the freeway seems one of the loveliest possible places to be. Each car is unique; each enters and leaves the stream of traffic according to individual goals and pursuits. None of us knows much about the rest of us. But each is influenced by the speed and attitude of those around. Each makes tiny adjustments to accommodate to the differences: you pull over to let me pass. I slow down to let you into the lane. We work together to get home.

Harmony is not being alike; in fact, it is intolerable to have someone driving next to you who maintains the exact speed and direction we do for any length of time. Sooner or later, one of us will feel compelled to speed up or slow down just to escape from that situation.

The "fallacy of composition" says that if a fire breaks out in a room I'm in and I run for the door, that's a wise procedure. But if a fire breaks out in a room we're all in, and we all run for the door, it is an unwise procedure. The pressure of all of us pushing against the door will make it impossible for any of us to get out.

If I decide to save $100 from each paycheck, that's a wise procedure. If we all decide to do the same thing, the economy will suffer a serious downturn. The differences between us make it possible for us to share the world in peace.

Watching the cars on the Oakland freeway merge into traffic then drive away, I glimpsed the beauty of the complexity of the universe. Just for a minute. Then my car overheated.

...and my highways will be raised up.

—*Isaiah 49:11*

ABOUT THE AUTHOR

As a teacher of English as a Second Language at the community college and adult school levels, Sharon Elwell was a "freeway flyer," one of the commuters who work part-time at several different school sites. All that driving time, she says, got her thinking about the application of Christian principles to experiences on the road. As she began collecting her meditations, *Driving Lessons* was born.

The mother of three daughters, mother-in-law of two "great guys," and grandmother of a three-year-old girl and a four-year-old boy, Sharon has published ESL and elementary school materials. This book represents her first collection of essays.

In her church life, Mrs. Elwell has taught almost every age group, but mostly teenagers. She currently serves as the accompanist in the children's Sunday school.

ORDER FORM

mp™

MERIWETHER PUBLISHING LTD.
P.O. BOX 7710
COLORADO SPRINGS, CO 80933
TELEPHONE: (719) 594-4422

Please send me the following books:

_____ **Driving Lessons #CC-B111** $10.95
by Sharon Elwell
Christian meditations about life in the
not-so-fast lane

_____ **The Official Sunday School Teachers** $9.95
Handbook #CC-B152
by Joanne Owens
An indispensable aid and barrel of laughs for anyone
involved in Sunday school activities

_____ **Divine Comedies #CC-B190** $12.95
by T.M. Williams
A collection of plays for church drama groups

_____ **Sermons Alive! #CC-B132** $12.95
by Paul Neale Lessard
52 dramatic sketches for worship services

_____ **Joy to the World! #CC-B161** $12.95
by L. G. Enscoe and Annie Enscoe
A variety collection of Christmas programs

_____ **The Best of the Jeremiah People #CC-B117** $14.95
by Jim Custer and Bob Hoose
Humorous skits and sketches by leading Christian repertory group

_____ **Teaching With Bible Games #CC-B108** $10.95
by Ed Dunlop
20 "kid-tested" contests for Christian education

These and other fine Meriwether Publishing books are available at
your local Christian bookstore or direct from the publisher. Use the
handy order form on this page.

NAME: _____

ORGANIZATION NAME: _____

ADDRESS: _____

CITY:_____ STATE: _____ ZIP: _____

PHONE: _____
□ **Check Enclosed**
□ **Visa or MasterCard #** _____
                                                    Expiration
Signature: _____ *Date:* _____
                    (required for Visa/Mastercard orders)

COLORADO RESIDENTS: Please add 3% sales tax.
SHIPPING: Include $2.75 for the first book and 50¢ for each additional book ordered.

□ *Please send me a copy of your complete catalog of books and plays.*